CLASSIC

classic

15 timeless designs to knit and keep forever

ERIKA KNIGHT
COLLECTABLES

photography by Katya de Grunwald

Quadrille

Editorial director Jane O'Shea
Creative director Helen Lewis
Designer Claire Peters
Project editor Lisa Pendreigh
Editorial assistant Andrew Bayliss
Pattern checker Eva Yates and Sally Harding
Photographer Katya de Grunwald
Photographer's assistant Amy Gwatkin
Stylist Beth Dadswell
Hair and make-up artist Anita Keeling
Model Amy Browne at Premier Model Management
Production director Vincent Smith
Production controller Bridget Fish

First published in 2006 by
Quadrille Publishing Limited
Alhambra House
27–31 Charing Cross Road
London WC2H 0LS
www.quadrille.co.uk

Text and project designs
  © 2006 Erika Knight
Photography
  © 2006 Katya de Grunwald
Design and layout
  © 2006 Quadrille Publishing Limited

British Library Cataloguing-in-Publication
Data: a catalogue record for this book is
available from the British Library.

ISBN-13 978 184400 327 3
ISBN-10 184400 327 2

Printed and bound in China

introduction

Classic is a staple collection of knitted wardrobe basics. Each garment has been considered, crafted and constructed to enhance and flatter the female form, creating highly wearable shapes that will work in myriad colourways and withstand the vagaries of fashion. Garments range from a quintessential round-neck cardigan to a practical V-neck tank top, an unstructured jacket to a perfect roll-neck sweater. Accessories include elegant gloves and scarf, as well as cosy socks. The range of yarns is natural, comfortable and eminently wearable: cotton, alpaca, merino, cashmere blends, linen and string. All the garments are worked in a flattering palette of ecru, soft blues, dusky pinks, muted greys, and, of course, basic black to underline the timeless appeal of the designs.

the
classic
collection

the
patterns

cable scarf

materials

Any medium-weight wool yarn, such as Rowan *RYC Cashsoft Aran*
  4 x 50g balls
Pair of 4.5mm knitting needles
2 stitch holders

size

One size, approximately 106.5cm long

tension

19 sts and 25 rows to 10cm over st st using 4.5mm needles

cable scarf

stitches

C6B (cable 6 back)

Slip next 3 sts onto cn and hold at back of work, k3, then k3 from cn.

C6F (cable 6 front)

Slip next 3 sts onto cn and hold at front of work, k3, then k3 from cn.

upwards cable

(worked over 12 sts)

Row 1 (RS): K.

Row 2: P.

Row 3: C6B, C6F.

Row 4: P.

Row 5: K.

Row 6: P.

Row 7: K.

Row 8: P.

downwards cable

(worked over 12 sts)

Row 1 (RS): K.

Row 2: P.

Row 3: C6F, C6B.

Row 4: P.

Row 5: K.

Row 6: P.

Row 7: K.

Row 8: P.

To make scarf

Using 4.5mm needles, cast on 50 sts.

Rib row 1 (RS): *K2, p1, rep from * to last 2 sts, k2.

Rib row 2: P2, *k1, p2, rep from * to end.

Rep last 2 rows twice.

Beg upwards cable patt as foll:

Next row (RS): [K1, p1] 3 times, k13, p1, work row 1 of upwards cable over next 12 sts, [p1, k1] 9 times.

Next row: [P1, k1] 9 times, work row 2 of upwards cable over next 12 sts, k1, p13, [k1, p1] 3 times.

Keeping rib and upwards cable pattern correct as set, cont in patt **and at the same time** working dec 3 sts in from edge, dec 1 st by working p2tog at end of next row and then at same edge on every foll 6th row until 38 sts rem, ending with WS facing for next row.

Next row (WS): [P1, k1] 3 times, p26, [k1, p1] 3 times.

Next row (RS): [K1, p1] 3 times, k26, [p1, k1] 3 times.

Cont in st st as now set, with 6-st rib border at each edge, until scarf measures 78.5cm from cast-on edge, ending with RS facing for next row. Beg shaping slit in scarf as foll:

Next row (RS): Rib 6, k12, p1, k2tog, k11, rib 6.

Next row: Rib 6, p12, then turn, leaving rem sts on a holder.

Work 18 rows in patt as set on these 18 sts.

Break off yarn and leave sts on a holder.

With WS facing, rejoin yarn to rem 19 sts left on first holder and work as foll:

Next row (WS): K1, work row 2 of downwards cable over next 12 sts, rib 6.

Next row: Rib 3, inc 1 in next st, rib 2, work row 3 of downwards cable over next 12 sts, p1.

Keeping downwards cable and rib sts correct as set, work 17 rows **and at the same time** inc 1 st at same edge of every foll 6th row.

Both sides of slit have now been completed.

Next row (RS): Rib 3, inc 1 in next st, rib 5, work row 5 of downwards cable over next 12 sts, p1, k into front and back of first st on holder, k next 11 sts from holder and then rib 6 from holder. *42 sts.*

Next row: Rib 6, p13, k1, p12, rib to end.

Cont as set, inc 1 st as set on same edge of every 6th row until there are 50 sts on needle.

Work 1 row (row 6 of downwards cable), ending with RS facing for next row.

Work 6 rows rib as for other end of scarf.

Cast off in rib.

To finish

Weave in any loose yarn ends. Gently steam to enhance the yarn, avoiding 'pressing' cable design. Pass end of scarf through slit to keep in place when worn.

casual sweater

materials

Any super-chunky-weight wool yarn, such as Debbie Bliss
  Cashmerino Superchunky
  8 (9: 10: 11: 12: 13) x 50g balls
Pair each of 7mm and 7.5mm knitting needles

sizes

dress size	8	10	12	14	16	18	
to fit bust	81	86	91	97	102	107	cm
actual bust	86	91	97	102	107	112	cm
length	53	57	60	62	65	67	cm
sleeve seam	42	42	43	43	44.5	46	cm

tension

12 sts and 17 rows to 10cm over st st using 7.5mm needles

pattern note

• After ribbing, work increases and decreases three stitches inside the
  edges to create a fully fashioned detail. Work the decreases
  through the back of loops as foll:
  On a k row: K3, k2tog, k to last 5 sts, k2tog tbl, k3.
  On a p row: P3, p2tog tbl, p to last 5 sts, p2tog, p3.

casual sweater

Back

Using 7mm needles, cast on 53 (58: 58: 63: 68: 68) sts.

Rib row 1 (RS): *K3, p2, rep from * to last 3 sts, k3.

Rib row 2: *P3, k2, rep from * to last 3 sts, p3.

Rep last 2 rows until back measures 5.5 (5.5: 5.5: 5.5: 8.5: 8.5)cm, ending with WS facing for next row.

Next row (WS): Rib as set, inc 1 st at end of row on sizes 8 and 18, dec 1 st at end of row on size 10, inc 1 st at each end of row on size 12, and dec 1 st at each end of row on size 16.
54 (57: 60: 63: 66: 69) sts.

Change to 7.5mm needles and beg with a K row, work in st st, dec 1 st at each end of 5th row and every foll 6th row until 46 (49: 52: 55: 58: 61) sts rem.

Cont in st st throughout, work 11 (13: 13: 13: 15: 15) rows straight, ending with RS facing for next row.

Inc 1 st at each end of next row and every foll 8th row until there are 52 (55: 58: 61: 64: 67) sts.

Cont straight until back measures 35 (38: 39.5: 40.5: 42: 43)cm from cast-on edge, ending with RS facing for next row.

Shape armholes

Cast off 3sts at beg of next 2 rows.
46 (49: 52: 55: 58: 61) sts.

Dec 1 st at each end of next and foll 3 (3: 3: 3: 4: 5) alt rows.
38 (41: 44: 47: 48: 49) sts.

Cont straight until armhole measures 18 (19: 20.5: 21.5: 23: 24)cm, ending with RS facing for next row.

Shape shoulders and neck

Next row (RS): Cast off 4 (4: 4: 6: 6: 6) sts, work until there are 7 (8: 9: 8: 9: 9) sts on right-hand needle, then turn, leaving rem sts unworked.

Cast off 3 sts at beg of next row.

Cast off rem 4 (5: 6: 5: 6: 6) sts.

With RS facing, rejoin yarn to rem sts and cast off centre 16 (17: 18: 19: 18: 19) sts, then complete to match first side, reversing all shaping.

Front

Work as for back until there are 10 (10: 10: 10: 12: 12) rows fewer worked than back to start of shoulder shaping, ending with RS facing for next row.

Shape neck

Next row (RS): K15 (16: 17: 19: 19: 19), then turn, leaving rem sts on a holder.

Work each side separately.

Cast off 3 sts at beg of next row.
12 (13: 14: 16: 16: 16) sts.

Dec 1 st at neck edge on next 3 rows and then on foll 1 (1: 1: 2: 1: 1) alt rows.
8 (9: 10: 11: 12: 12) sts.

Work 3 (3: 3: 1: 5: 5) rows straight, ending with RS facing for next row.

Shape shoulders

Cast off 4 (4: 4: 6: 6: 6) sts at beg of next row.

Work 1 row straight.

Cast off rem 4 (5: 6: 5: 6: 6) sts.

With RS facing, rejoin yarn to rem sts and cast off centre 8 (9: 10: 9: 10: 11) sts, then complete to match first side, reversing all shaping.

Sleeves

Using 7mm needles, cast on 30 (30: 30: 35: 35: 35) sts.

Rib row 1 (RS): *K3, p2, rep from * to end.

Rib row 2: *K2, p3, rep from * to end.

Rep last 2 rows until rib measures 10 (10: 10: 10: 12.5: 12.5)cm from cast-on edge, ending with WS facing for next row.

Next row (WS): Rib as set, inc 3 sts across row on size 12, and inc 1 st at end of row on sizes 16 and 18. *30 (30: 33: 35: 36: 36) sts.*

Change to 7.5mm needles and beg with a k row, work in st st, inc 1 st at each end of 5th row and every foll 8th row until there are 40 (42: 45: 45: 46: 48) sts.

Cont in st st throughout, work straight until sleeve measures 42 (42: 43: 43: 44.5: 46)cm from cast-on edge, ending with RS facing for next row.

Shape top

Cast off 3 (3: 3: 3: 3: 3) sts at beg of next 2 rows.

Dec 1 st at each end of next row and every foll alt row until 26 (28: 29: 29: 30: 32) sts rem.

Dec 1 st at each end of foll 4th row. *24 (26: 27: 27: 28: 30) sts.*

Work 3 rows straight.

Dec 1 st at each end of next row and foll alt row, then on foll 3 rows.

Cast off 3 sts at beg of next 2 rows.

Cast off rem 10 (12: 13: 13: 14: 15) sts.

Collar

Sew right shoulder seam.

Using 7mm needles and with RS facing, pick up and k 14 (14: 13: 13: 16: 16) sts down left side of front neck, 8 (9: 10: 9: 10: 11) sts across centre front, 14 (14: 13: 13: 16: 16) sts up right side of front neck, and 22 (23: 24: 25: 24: 25) sts across back neck. *58 (60: 60: 60: 66: 68) sts.*

Sizes 8 and 18 only

Next row: K2, p3, k into front and back of next st, [p3, k2] twice, p3, k into front and back of next st, p3, *k2, p3, rep from * to end. *60 (–: –: –: –: 70) sts.*

Size 16 only

Next row: K2tog, k1, *p3, k2, rep from * to last 3 sts, p3. *– (–: –: –: 65: –) sts.*

All sizes

Next row: *K3, p2, rep from * to end.

Work 10cm in rib as set.

Cast off in rib.

To finish

Weave in any loose yarn ends.

Lay work out flat and gently steam to enhance the yarn.

Sew collar and shoulder seam.

Sew sleeve heads into armholes.

Sew side and sleeve seams.

postman's bag

materials

Any medium-weight cotton parcel string
   9 x 80m balls
Pair of 4.5mm knitting needles
Piece of leather, approximately 7.5cm by 13cm, for handle
2 large buttons, 2 medium-size buttons and 2 large press studs

size

One size, approximately 33cm by 26.5cm

tension

14 sts and 24 rows to 10cm over moss st using 4.5mm needles

Back
Using 4.5mm needles, cast on 47 sts.
Row 1: K1, *p1, k1, rep from * to end.
Rep last row to form moss st and keeping moss st patt correct as set throughout, work 64 rows, dec 1 st at each end of rows 21 and 42. *43 sts.***
Mark each end of last row to mark fold line of front flap.
Work 55 rows, inc 1 st at each end of row 21. *45 sts.*
Cast off in moss st.

Front
Work as for back to **.
Cast off in moss st.

Straps (make 2)
Using 4.5mm needles, cast on 17 sts.
Working in moss st as for back and keeping patt correct as set throughout, work 39 rows.
Mark each end of last row to mark bottom corner of bag.
Dec 1 st at each end of every foll 16th row until 11 sts rem.
Work 16 rows straight.
Mark each end of last row to mark corner of bag.
Work 113 rows, dec 1 st at each end of row 20. *9 sts.*
Cast off in moss st.

To finish
Weave in any loose yarn ends.
Working all seams as external seams, sew cast-on edges of straps together to form centre bottom of gusset of bag.
Sew front and back to strap between markers, allowing flap to fold to front.
Sew large buttons to front flap and press studs underneath.
Sew one medium-size button to each strap end.
Trim leather to width of strap and cut a buttonhole at each end.
Button leather strip onto straps.

wraparound jacket

materials

Any super-chunky-weight wool yarn, such as Rowan *Spray*
  10 (11: 12) x 100g balls
Pair of 10mm knitting needles

sizes

dress size	8–10	12–14	16–18	
to fit bust	81–86	91–97	102–107	cm
actual bust	106	117	127	cm
length	63.5	68.5	73.5	cm
sleeve seam	46	47	48	cm

tension

9 sts and 12 rows to 10cm over st st using 10mm needles

wraparound jacket

pattern notes

- As the row-end edges of the fronts form the actual finished edge of the garment, it is important that all new balls of yarn are joined in at the side seam or the armhole edges of rows.
- Work increases and decreases three stitches inside the edges to create a fully fashioned detail. Work the decreases through the back of loops as foll:

On a k row: K3, k2tog, k to last 5 sts, k2tog tbl, k3.
On a p row: P3, p2tog tbl, p to last 5 sts, p2tog, p3.

Back

Using 10mm needles, cast on 48 (52: 56) sts.
Rib row 1 (RS): *K1, p1, rep from * to end.
Rep last row once.
Beg with a k row, work in st st until back measures 42 (44.5: 47)cm from cast-on edge, ending with RS facing for next row.

Shape armhole

Cast off 3 sts at beg of next 2 rows. *42 (46: 50) sts.*
Dec 1 st at each end of next 3 rows. *36 (40: 44) sts.*
Cont straight until armhole measures 21.5 (24: 26.5)cm, ending with RS facing for next row.

Shape shoulders

Cast off 4 (5: 5) sts at beg of next 2 rows and 5 (5: 6) sts at beg of foll 2 rows. *18 (20: 22) sts.*
Work 15cm in k1, p1 rib.
Cast off in rib.

Right front

Using 10mm needles, cast on 40 (44: 48) sts.
Work 2 rows in rib as for back.
Next row (RS): [K1, p1] 9 times, k to end.
Next row: P to last 18 sts, [k1, p1] 9 times.
Rep last 2 rows until front measures 34.5 (37: 39.5)cm from cast-on edge, ending with RS facing for next row.

Add 2 extra sts into rib section as foll:
Next row (RS): [K1, p1] 10 times, k to end.
Cont to add 2 extra sts into rib section on every foll 8th row until 26 (28: 30) sts are being ribbed **and at the same time** when work measures 42 (44.5: 47)cm from cast-on edge, ending with WS facing for next row, shape armhole as foll:

Shape armhole

Cast off 3 sts at beg of row. *37 (41: 45) sts.*
Dec 1 st at armhole edge of next 3 rows. *34 (38: 42) sts.*
Cont straight until armhole measures 21.5 (24: 26.5)cm, ending

with WS facing for next row.
Shape shoulder
Cast off 4 (5: 5) sts at beg of next row
and 5 (5: 6) sts at beg of foll alt row.
25 (28: 31) sts.
Work 15cm in k1, p1 rib.
Cast off in rib.

Left front
Using 10mm needles, cast on 40
(44: 48) sts.
Work 2 rows in rib as for back.
Next row (RS): K to last 17 sts,
[p1, k1] 8 times, p1.
Next row: K1, [p1, k1] 8 times,
p to end.
Rep last 2 rows until front measures
34.5 (37: 39.5)cm from cast-on

edge, ending with RS facing for
next row.
Add 2 extra sts into rib section as
foll:
Next row: K to last 19 sts, [p1, k1]
9 times, p1.
Complete to match right front,
reversing all shaping, but increasing
rib section to only 25 (27: 29) sts.

Sleeves (make 2)
Cast on 30 (30: 32) sts.
Work 10cm in k1, p1 rib.
Beg with a k, work in st st, inc 1 st at
each end of 7th row and every foll
8th row until there are 38 (42: 46) sts.
Cont in st st throughout, work
straight until sleeve measures 46

(47: 48)cm from cast-on edge,
ending with RS facing for next row.
Shape top
Cast off 3 sts at beg of next 2 rows.
32 (36: 40) sts.
Dec 1 st at each end next row and
foll 3 alt rows.
24 (28: 32) sts.
Work 1 row straight.
Cast off.

To finish
Weave in any loose yarn ends.
Gently steam to enhance the yarn.
Sew shoulder and collar seams.
Sew sleeve heads to armholes.
Sew side and sleeve seams.

military cardigan

materials

Any lightweight wool yarn, such as Rowan *Tapestry*
8 (9: 9: 10: 11: 11) x 50g balls
Pair each of 3.75mm and 4mm knitting needles
13 buttons
9 press studs

sizes

dress size	8	10	12	14	16	18	
to fit bust	81	86	91	97	102	107	cm
actual bust	86	92	97	103	108	114	cm
length	51	53	56	58.5	61	61	cm
sleeve seam	46	46	48.5	48.5	48.5	49.5	cm

tension

24 sts and 32 rows to 10cm over st st using 4mm needles.

pattern notes

• As row edges of fronts form actual finished edges of garment, it is important that all new balls of yarn are joined in at side seam or armhole edges of rows.
• Work increases and decreases at armholes, neck and on pocket flaps three stitches inside the edges to create a fully fashioned detail. Work the decreases through the back of loops as foll:
On a k row: K3, k2tog, k to last 5 sts, k2tog tbl, k3.
On a p row: P3, p2tog tbl, p to last 5 sts, p2tog, p3.

military cardigan

Back

Using 3.75mm needles, cast on 105 (110: 115: 120: 125: 135) sts.

Rib row 1 (RS): *K3, p2, rep from * to end.

Rib row 2: *K2, p3, rep from * to end.

Rep last 2 rows until back measures 7cm, ending with WS facing for next row.

Next row (WS): Rib as set, dec 1 st at each end of row on sizes 8 and 18, dec 1 st at end of row on size 10, inc 1 st at end of row on size 14, and inc 1 st at each end of row on size 16.
103 (109: 115: 121: 127: 133) sts.

Change to 4mm needles and st st and cont straight until back measures 32 (33: 34: 36: 37: 37)cm, ending with RS facing for next row.

Shape armholes

Cast off 6 sts at beg of next 2 rows, then dec 1 st at each end of foll 5 rows and then foll 4 alt rows.
73 (79: 85: 91: 97: 103) sts.

Cont straight until armhole measures 17.5 (19: 20: 20: 21.5: 23)cm, ending with RS facing for next row.

Shape shoulder and neck

Cast off 6 (6: 7: 8: 8: 9) sts at beg of next 2 rows.

Next row (RS): Cast off 5 (6: 7: 8: 9: 10) sts, work until there are 9 (11: 11: 12: 13: 14) sts on right needle, turn.

Cast off 4 sts at beg of next row.

Cast off rem 5 (7: 7: 8: 9: 10) sts.

With RS facing, rejoin yarn to rem sts and cast off centre 33 (33: 35: 35: 37: 37) sts, then k to end.

Complete to match first side, reversing all shaping.

Right front

Using 3.75mm needles, cast on 60 (60: 65: 70: 70: 75) sts.

Rib row 1 (RS): [K1, p1] 5 times, *k3, p2, rep from * to end.

Rib row 2: *K2, p3, rep from * to last 10 sts, [k1, p1] 5 times.

Rep last 2 rows until front measures 7cm, ending with WS facing for next row.

Next row (WS): Rib as set, dec 1 st at beg of row on sizes 8 and 18, inc 1 st at beg and middle of row on size 10, dec 1 st at beg and middle of row on size 14, and inc 1 st at beg of row on size 16.
59 (62: 65: 68: 71: 74) sts.

Change to 4mm needles and keeping 10 k1, p1 rib sts as set for button band, cont in st st until front measures same as back to armhole, ending with WS facing for next row.

Shape armhole

Cast off 6 sts at beg of next row, then dec 1 st at armhole edge of foll 5 rows and every foll alt row 4 times.
44 (47: 50: 53: 56: 59) sts.

Cont straight until front measures 5 (5: 5: 5: 5: 5.5: 5.5)cm less than back to shoulder, ending with RS facing for next row.

Shape neck

Next row (RS): Rib first 10 sts and leave on a holder, cast off next 7 (7: 9: 9: 9: 9) sts, k to end.

Cast off 4 sts at beg of next alt row, then dec 1 st at neck edge on foll 3 rows and then on every foll alt row until there are 16 (19: 21: 24: 26: 29) sts.

Work straight until front measures same as back to shoulder, ending with WS facing for next row.

Cast off 6 (6: 7: 8: 8: 9) sts at beg of next row and 5 (6: 7: 8: 9: 10) sts at beg of foll alt row.

Work 1 row straight.

Cast off rem 5 (7: 7: 8: 9: 10) sts.

Left front

Using 3.75mm needles, cast on 60 (60: 65: 70: 70: 75) sts.

Row 1 (RS): *K3, p2, rep from * to last 10 sts, [k1, p1] 5 times.

Row 2: [K1, p1] 5 times, *k2, p3, rep from * to end.

Rep last 2 rows until front measures 7cm, ending with WS facing for next row.

Next row (WS): Rib as set, dec 1 st at end of row on sizes 8 and 18, inc 1 st at middle and end of row on size 10, dec 1 st at middle

of and end of row on size 14, and inc 1 st at end of row on size 16. *59 (62: 65: 68: 71: 74) sts.*
Change to 4mm needles and keeping 10 k1, p1 rib sts as set for button band, cont in st st and complete as for right front, reversing all shaping.

Sleeve (make 2)
Using 3.75mm needles, cast on 55 (55: 55: 60: 60: 60) sts.
Row 1 (RS): *K3, p2, rep from * to end.
Row 2: *K2, p3, rep from * to end.
Rep last 2 rows until sleeve measures 14cm ending with RS facing for next row.
Change to 4mm needles and beg with a k row, work in st st, inc 1 st at each end of 7th row and every foll 8th row until there are 77 (79: 79: 82: 84: 88) sts.
Cont straight until sleeve measures 46 (46: 48.5: 48.5: 49.5)cm from cast-on edge, ending with RS facing for next row.

Shape top
Cast off 5 sts at beg of next 2 rows, then dec 1 st at each end of foll 5 rows and every foll alt row until 25 (27: 27: 30: 32: 36) sts rem.
Dec 1 st at each end of next 5 rows.
Cast off rem 15 (17: 17: 20: 22: 26) sts.

Pockets (make 2)
Using 4mm needles, cast on 20 (20: 20: 23: 23: 23) sts.
Row 1 (RS): P1, k1, p1, k to last 3 sts, p1, k1, p1.
Row 2: K1, p1, k1, p to last 3 sts, k1, p1, k1.
Row 3: P1, k1, p1, m1, k to last 3 sts, m1, p1, k1, p1.
Row 4: K1, p1, k1, p to last 3 sts, k1, p1, k1.
Rep last 2 rows twice.
26 (26: 26: 29: 29: 29) sts.
Keeping rib patt correct as set, cont straight until pocket measures 11.5 (11.5: 11.5: 13: 13: 13)cm from cast-on edge.
Cast off.

Pocket tops (make 2)
Using 4mm needles, cast on 28 (28: 28: 31: 31: 31) sts.
Rep rows 1 and 2 of pocket 3 times.
Keeping patt correct as set, dec 1 st at each end of every row (inside rib sts) until 8 sts rem, ending with RS facing for next row.
Next row: P1, k1, k2tog, k2tog tbl, k1, p1.
Next row: K1, p2tog tbl, p2tog, k1. *4 sts.*
Next row: K2tog, k2tog tbl. *2 sts.*
Next row: P2tog and fasten off.

Epaulettes (make 2)
Using 3.75mm needles, cast on 10 sts.

Work 10cm in k1, p1 rib.
Cast off in rib.

To finish
Weave in any loose yarn ends.
Gently steam with care.
Sew both shoulder seams.

Collar
Using 3.75mm needles and with RS facing, rib 10 sts from holder as set, pick up and k 25 (25: 27: 27: 29: 29) sts along right front neck, 42 (42: 43: 43: 44: 44) sts across centre back, 25 (25: 27: 27: 29: 29) sts along left front neck, and rib 10 sts from holder.
112 (112: 117: 117: 123: 123) sts.
Next row (WS): Rib 10 sts, *k2, p3, rep from * to last 12 sts, k2, rib 10 sts.
Work in rib patt as set until collar measures 8cm.
Cast off in rib.
Sew sleeve heads to armholes.
Sew side and sleeve seams.
Sew on pockets above ribbing, then sew on flaps.
Sew cast-on edge of epaulettes to armhole seam. Sew one button to each pocket flap and end of each epaulette, securing epaulettes in place at same time. Sew rem buttons evenly spaced along front bands and collar. Sew on press studs under under buttons on front band.

tank top

materials

Any super-chunky-weight wool yarn, such as Rowan *Big Wool*
   3 (3: 3: 4: 4: 5) x 100g balls
Pair each of 10mm and 12mm knitting needles

sizes

dress size	8	10	12	14	16	18	
to fit bust	81	86	91	97	102	107	cm
actual bust	81	86	91	97	102	107	cm
length	44.5	47	49.5	52	54	57	cm

tension

18 sts and 12 rows to 10cm over st st using 12mm needles

tank top

pattern note

• To create a fully fashioned detail, work increases and decreases two or three stitches inside the edges as instructed.

Back

Using 10mm needles, cast on 33 (33: 36: 39: 39: 42) sts.

Rib row 1 (RS): *K2, p1, rep from * to end.

Rib row 2: *K1, p2, rep from * to end.

Rep last 2 rows until back measures 15 (17: 17: 18: 18: 19)cm from cast-on edge, ending with WS facing for next row.

Next row (WS): Rib as set, dec 1 st at beg of row on sizes 8 and 14, and inc 1 st at beg of row on sizes 10 and 16.

*32 (34: 36: 38: 40: 42) sts.***

Change to 12mm needles and beg with a k row, work in st st until back measures 27.5 (29: 30.5: 32: 32: 34)cm from cast-on edge, ending with RS facing for next row.

Shape armhole

Cont in st st throughout, cast off 2 sts at beg of next 2 rows.

28 (30: 32: 34: 36: 38) sts.

Next row (RS): K2, k2tog, k to last 4 sts, k2tog tbl, k2.

Next row: P.

Rep last 2 rows once more.

24 (26: 28: 30: 32: 34) sts.

Cont straight until armhole measures 17 (18: 19: 20: 22: 23)cm, ending with RS facing for next row.

Shape shoulders and neck

Next row (RS): Cast off 4 (4: 4: 4: 5: 5) sts, k until there are 4 (4: 5: 5: 5: 5) sts on right-hand needle, then turn.

Cast off rem 4 (4: 5: 5: 5: 5) sts.

With RS facing, rejoin yarn to rem sts and cast off centre 8 (10: 10: 12: 12: 14) sts, then k to end.

Complete to match first side, reversing all shaping.

Front

Work as for back to **.

Change to 12mm needles and beg with a k row, work 4 (4: 4: 6: 6: 6) rows in st st.

Next row (RS): K16 (17: 18: 19: 20: 21), then turn, leaving rem sts on a holder.

Shape neck

Next row (WS): K1, p1, k1, p to end.

Next row: K to last 3 sts, p1, k1, p1.

Next row: K1, p1, k1, p to end.

Rep last 2 rows once more.

Next row (dec row) (RS): K to last 5 sts, k2tog tbl, p1, k1, p1.

Cont in st st with 3-st rib border, dec 1 st inside 3-st rib border as set on every foll 4th row **and at the same time** when front same as back to armhole, shape armhole as for back.

Cont dec at neck edge on every 4th row until 8 (8: 9: 9: 10: 10) sts rem.

Cont straight until armhole measures same as back to shoulder, ending with RS facing for next row.

Shape shoulder

Cast off 4 (4: 4: 4: 5: 5) sts at beg of next row.

Cast off rem 4 (4: 5: 5: 5: 5) sts.

With RS facing, rejoin yarn to rem sts and complete to match first side, reversing all shaping.

To finish

Weave in any loose yarn ends.

Lay work out flat and gently steam.

Sew shoulder seams with a flat seam.

Sew side seams.

bardot sweater

materials

Any super-chunky-weight wool yarn, such as Rowan *Little Big Wool*
11 (12: 12: 13: 14: 14) x 100g balls
Pair each of 9mm and 10mm knitting needles

sizes

dress size	8	10	12	14	16	18	
to fit bust	81	86	91	97	102	107	cm
actual bust	91.5	99	107	114.5	122	127	cm
length	47	49.5	52	54	57	59.5	cm
sleeve seam	44.5	44.5	47	47	49.5	49.5	cm

tension

14 sts and 14 rows to 10cm over rib using 10mm needles

bardot sweater

pattern note

• To create a fully fashioned detail, work decreases two stitches in from edge if desired.

Back

Using 9mm needles, cast on 63 (68: 73: 78: 83: 88) sts.

Row 1 (RS): *K3, p2, rep from * to last 3 sts, k3.

Row 2: *P3, k2, rep from * to last 3 sts, p3.

Rep last 2 rows 3 times more.
Change to 10mm needles and cont in rib as set until back measures 30.5 (32: 33: 34.5: 36: 37)cm from cast-on edge, ending with RS facing for next row.

Shape raglan armhole

Keeping rib patt correct as set throughout, cast off 3 sts at beg of next 2 rows.

57 (62: 67: 72: 77: 82) sts.
Dec 1 st at each end of next 5 rows, then on foll alt row.
45 (50: 55: 60: 65: 70) sts.
Cont straight until back measures 47 (49.5: 52: 54: 57: 59.5)cm from cast-on edge, ending with RS facing for next row.
Cast off in rib.

Front

Work as for back until 4 (4: 4: 6: 6: 6) rows fewer have been worked before cast off.

Next row (RS): Work 14 (16: 18: 20: 22: 24) sts, then turn, leaving rem sts on a holder.

Cast off 2 sts at beg of next row and foll alt row.
10 (12: 14: 16: 18: 20) sts.
Work 0 (0: 0: 2: 2: 2) rows straight.
Cast off in rib.
With RS facing, rejoin yarn to rem sts and cast off centre 17 (18: 19: 20: 21: 22) sts, then work to end.
Complete to match first side, reversing all shaping.

Sleeves (make 2)

Using 9mm needles, cast on 33 (33: 38: 38: 43: 43) sts.
Work 8 rows in rib as for back.
Change to 10mm needles and keeping rib correct as set

throughout, inc 1 st at each end of next row and every foll 12th row until there are 43 (43: 48: 48: 53: 53) sts, work extra sts into rib. Cont straight until sleeve measures 44.5 (44.5: 47: 47: 49.5: 49.5)cm from cast-on edge, ending with RS facing for next row.

Shape raglan armhole
Cast off 3 sts at beg of next 2 rows.
37 (37: 42: 42: 47: 47) sts.
Dec 1 st at each end of next 2 rows, then on next and foll 3 (3: 4: 4: 4: 4) alt rows, then on foll 4th row 2 (2: 2: 2: 3: 3) times.
21 (21: 24: 24: 27: 27) sts.
Work 3 (3: 5: 7: 7: 9) rows straight.

Cast off in rib.

To finish
Sew both front and right back raglan seams.

Collar
Using 9mm needles and with RS facing, pick up and k 19 (19: 22: 22: 25: 25) sts across top of left sleeve, 14 (14: 15: 15: 16: 16) sts down left front neck, 17 (18: 19: 20: 21: 22) sts across centre front neck, 14 (14: 15: 15: 16: 16) sts up right front neck, 19 (19: 22: 22: 25: 25) sts across top of right sleeve, and 44 (48: 54: 58: 64: 68) sts across back neck.
127 (132: 147: 152: 167: 172) sts.

Row 1: *K3, p2, rep from * to last 2 sts, k2.
Row 2: P2, *k2, p3, rep from * to end.
Rep last 2 rows until collar measures 15cm, then change to 10mm needles and work 15cm more.
Cast off in rib.
Sew raglan and collar seam, reversing seam for last 15cm of collar.
Sew sleeve and side seams.

kelly cardigan

materials

Any fine-weight mohair yarn, such as Rowan *Kidsilk Haze*
  6 (6: 8: 8: 10: 10) x 25g balls
Pair each of 3mm and 3.75mm knitting needles
9 press studs

sizes

dress size	8	10	12	14	16	18	
to fit bust	81	86	91	97	102	107	cm
actual bust	86	92	97	103	108	114	cm
length	47	48	49	50	51	52	cm
sleeve seam	36	36	37	37	37	38	cm

tension

22 sts and 30 rows to 10cm over st st using 3.75mm needles and
  yarn double

pattern notes

• Remember to use two strands of the yarn together throughout.
• To create a fully fashioned detail, work increases and decreases
  three sts inside the edges as instructed.
• Work the front k1, p1 rib buttonbands integrally with each front
  to give a neater finish and to avoid having to sew it on.

kelly cardigan

Back

Using 3mm needles and two strands of yarn tog, cast on 87 (95: 101: 107: 113: 119) sts.

Rib row 1 (RS): *P1, k1, rep from * to last st, p1.

Rib row 2: *K1, p1, rep from * to last st, k1

Rep last 2 rows until back measures 5cm from cast-on edge, ending with RS facing for next row.

Change to 3.75mm needles.

Next row (RS): K3, m1, k to last 3 sts, m1, k3.

Cont in st st throughout, inc 1 st in same way at each end of every foll 20th row until there are 95 (101: 107: 113: 119: 125) sts.

Cont straight until back measures 29 (30: 30: 31: 31: 32)cm from cast-on edge, ending with RS facing for next row.

Shape armholes

Cast off 4 (5: 5: 6: 6: 7) sts at beg of next 2 rows and 3 sts at beg of foll 2 rows.

81 (85: 91: 95: 101: 105) sts.

Next row (RS): K3, k2tog, k to last 5 sts, k2tog tbl, k3.

Next row: P3, p2tog tbl, p to last 5 sts, p2tog tbl, p3.

Dec 1 st in same way at each end of next 1 (1: 3: 3: 5: 5) rows and then on foll 0 (1: 1: 2: 2: 3) alt rows and then on foll 4th row.

73 (75: 77: 79: 81: 83) sts.

Cont straight until armhole measures 18 (18: 19: 19: 20: 20)cm, ending with RS facing for next row.

Shape shoulders and neck

Cast off 7 (7: 7: 7: 8: 8) sts at beg of next 2 rows.

59 (61: 63: 65: 65: 67) sts.

Next row (RS): Cast off 7 (7: 7: 7: 8: 8) sts, k until there are 10 (10: 11: 11: 10: 11) sts on right-hand needle, then turn, leaving rem sts on a holder.

Work this side first.

Cast off 3 sts at beg of next row.

Cast off rem 7 (7: 8: 8: 7: 8) sts.

With RS facing, rejoin yarn to rem sts and cast off centre 25 (27: 27: 29: 29: 29) sts, then k to end.

Complete to match first side, reversing all shaping.

Left front

Using 3mm needles and two strands of yarn tog, cast on 53 (55: 59: 61: 65: 67) sts.

Rep 2 rib rows as for back until front measures 5cm from cast-on edge, ending with RS facing for next row and inc 0 (1: 0: 1: 0: 1) st at end (side-seam edge) of last row.

53 (56: 59: 62: 65: 68) sts.

Change to 3.75mm needles.

Next row (RS): K3, m1, k to last 5 sts, [p1, k1] twice, p1.

Cont in st st throughout, with 5-st rib border as set, inc 1 st at side-seam edge on every foll 20th row until there are 56 (59: 62: 65: 68: 71) sts.

Cont straight until front measures 29 (30: 30: 31: 31: 32)cm from cast-on edge, ending with RS facing for next row.

Shape armhole

Cast off 4 (5: 5: 6: 6: 7) sts at beg of next row and 3 sts at beg of foll alt row.

49 (51: 54: 56: 59: 61) sts.

Work 1 row straight.

Working all armhole decreases as set for back, dec 1 st at armhole edge of next 3 (3: 5: 5: 7: 7) rows, then on foll 0 (1: 1: 2: 2: 3) alt rows, then on foll 4th row.

45 (46: 47: 48: 49: 50) sts.

Cont straight until 11 (11: 11: 11: 11: 13) rows fewer have been worked than for back to start of shoulder shaping, ending with WS facing for next row.

Shape neck

Next row (WS): Rib first 5 sts and leave on a holder, cast off next 8 (9: 9: 10: 10: 11) sts, p to end. Cast off 4 sts at beg of foll alt row. *28 (28: 29: 29: 30: 30) sts.*
Working decreases as before, dec 1 st at neck edge on next 7 rows, then on foll 0 (0: 0: 0: 0: 1) alt rows. *21 (21: 22: 22: 23: 24) sts.*
Work 1 row straight, ending with RS facing for next row.

Shape shoulder

Cast off 7 (7: 7: 7: 8: 8) sts at beg of next and foll alt row.
Work 1 row straight.
Cast off rem 7 (7: 8: 8: 7: 8) sts.

Right front

Work as for left front, reversing all shaping and working 1 extra row before start of armhole shaping.

Sleeves (make 2)

Using 3mm needles and two strands of yarn tog, cast on 53 (53: 55: 57: 57: 59) sts.
Work 3cm in k1, p1 rib.

Change to 3.75mm needles.
Beg with a k row, work in st st throughout, inc 1 st at each end of 7th row and every foll 12th (10th: 10th: 8th: 8th: 10th) row until there are 69 (67: 67: 69: 61: 79) sts.

Sizes 10, 12, 14 and 16 only

Inc 1 st at each end of every foll – (12th: 12th: 12th: 10th: –) row until there are – (71: 73: 75: 77: –) sts.

All sizes

69 (71: 73: 75: 77: 79) sts.
Cont straight until sleeve measures 36 (36: 37: 37: 37: 38)cm from cast-on edge, ending with RS facing for next row.

Shape top

Cast off 4 (5: 5: 6: 6: 7) sts at beg of next 2 rows and 3 sts at beg of foll 2 rows.
55 (55: 57: 57: 59: 59) sts.
Dec 1 st at each end of next 3 rows and foll 2 alt rows, then on every foll 4th row until 35 (35: 37: 37: 39: 39) sts rem.
Work 1 row straight, ending with RS facing for next row.
Dec 1 st at each end of next and every foll alt rows until 29 sts rem, then on foll row, ending with RS facing for next row.

27 sts.
Cast off 3 sts at beg of next 4 rows.
Cast off rem 15 sts.

To finish

Weave in any loose yarn ends.
Steam garment gently.
Sew shoulder seams.
Sew sleeve heads to armholes.
Sew sleeve and side seams.

Neckband

Using 3mm needles and two strands of yarn tog, and with RS facing, rib 5 from right front holder, pick up k 18 (19: 19: 21: 21: 21) sts up right front neck, 31 (33: 33: 35: 35: 35) sts across back neck, and 18 (19: 19: 21: 21: 21) sts down left front neck, then rib 5 from holder. *77 (81: 81: 87: 87: 87) sts.*
Work 2.5cm in k1, p1 rib as set by front bands.
Cast off in rib.
Sew press studs, evenly spaced, to inside of front bands, including neckband.

'mademoiselle' jacket

materials

Any medium-weight silk-blend yarn, such as Rowan *RYC Natural Silk Aran*
  12 (13: 14: 15: 16: 17) x 50g balls
Pair each of 4mm and 4.5mm knitting needles
Approximately 3m of narrow ribbon in each of two colours

sizes

dress size	8	10	12	14	16	18	
to fit bust	81	86	91	97	102	107	cm
actual bust	86	92	97	103	108	114	cm
length	47	48	49	50	51	52	cm
sleeve seam	38	39.5	39.5	39.5	42	42	cm

tension

19 sts and 25 rows to 10cm over st st using 4.5mm needles

'mademoiselle' jacket

pattern notes

- Work increases and decreases at armholes, neck and on pockets three stitches inside the edges to create a fully fashioned detail. Work the decreases through the back of loops as foll:
  On a k row: K3, k2tog, k to last 5 sts, k2tog tbl, k3.
  On a p row: P3, p2tog tbl, p to last 5 sts, p2tog, p3.
- As row edges of fronts form actual finished edge of garment, it is important that all new balls of yarn are joined in at side seam or armhole edges of rows.

Back

Using 4mm needles, cast on 72 (76: 80: 84: 88: 92) sts.

K 4 rows.

Change to 4.5mm needles and cont in st st with rib borders for side slits as foll:

Next row (RS): P1, k1, p1, m1, k to last 3 sts, m1, p1, k1, p1.

Next row: K1, p1, k1, p to last 3 sts, k1, p1, k1.

Rep last 2 rows 3 times more.

80 (84: 88: 92: 96: 100) sts.

This completes side-slit borders.

Cont in st st only throughout, dec 1 st at each end of 7th row and every foll 7th (8th: 8th: 8th: 9th: 9th) row until 74 (78: 82: 86: 90: 94) sts rem.

Work 15 (17: 17: 19: 19: 19) rows straight, ending with RS facing for next row.

Inc 1 st at each end of next row and every foll 7th (8th: 8th: 9th: 9th: 9th) row until there are 80 (84: 88: 92: 96: 100) sts.

Cont straight until back measures 29 (29: 29: 28.5: 28: 28)cm from cast-on edge, ending with RS facing for next row.

Shape armholes

Cast off 4 (4: 4: 5: 5: 5) sts at beg of next 2 rows.

72 (76: 80: 82: 86; 90) sts.

Dec 1 st at each end of next 3 (3: 3: 3: 4: 4) rows, then on foll 2 alt rows.

62 (66: 70: 72: 74: 78) sts.

Cont straight until armhole measures 18 (19: 20: 21.5: 23: 24)cm, ending with RS facing for next row.

Shape shoulders and neck

Cast off 5 (6: 6: 6: 6: 7) sts at beg of next 2 rows.

52 (54: 58: 60: 62: 64) sts.

Next row (RS): Cast off 5 (6: 7: 6: 7: 7) sts, k until there are 9 (9: 9: 10: 10: 11) sts on right-hand needle, then turn, leaving rem sts on a holder.

Cast off 3 sts at beg of next row.

Cast off rem 6 (6: 6: 7: 7: 8) sts.

With RS of work facing, rejoin yarn to rem sts and cast off centre 24 (24: 26: 28: 28: 28) sts, then k to end.

Complete to match first side, reversing all shaping.

Right front

Using 4mm needles, cast on 36 (38: 40: 42: 44: 46) sts.

K 4 rows.

Change to 4.5mm needles and cont in st st with rib borders as foll:

Next row (RS): P1, k1, p1, k to last 3 sts, m1, p1, k1, p1.

Next row: K1, p1, k1, p to last 3 sts, k1, p1, k1.

Rep last 2 rows 3 times.

40 (42: 44: 46: 48: 50) sts.

This completes side-slit border.

Cont in st st throughout and keeping 3 rib sts as set along centre front only (beg of RS rows and end of WS rows), dec 1 st at side edge only on 7th row and every foll 7th (8th: 8th: 8th: 9th: 9th) row until 37 (39: 41: 43: 45: 47) sts rem.

Work 15 (17: 17: 19: 19: 19) rows straight, ending with RS facing for next row.

Inc 1 st at side edge on next row and every foll 7th (8th: 8th: 9th: 9th: 9th) row until there are 40 (42: 44: 46: 48: 50) sts.

Cont straight until front measures 29 (29: 29: 28.5: 28: 28)cm from cast-on edge, ending with WS facing for next row.

Shape armhole

Cast off 4 (4: 4: 5: 5: 5) sts at beg of row.

36 (38: 40: 41: 43: 45) sts.

Dec 1 st at armhole edge of next 3 rows, then on foll 2 alt rows.

31 (33: 35: 36: 38: 40) sts.

Cont straight until armhole measures

11 (11: 12.5: 14: 14.5: 15)cm, ending with RS facing for next row.

Shape neck

Cast off 6 (6: 7: 7: 8: 8) sts at beg of next row.

25 (27: 28: 29: 30: 32) sts.

Dec 1 st at neck edge of next 7 rows, then on foll 2 (2: 2: 3: 3: 3) alt rows.

16 (18: 19: 19: 20: 22) sts.

Cont straight until armhole matches back to shoulder shaping, ending at armhole edge.

Shape shoulder

Cast off 5 (6: 6: 6: 6: 7) sts at beg of next row and 5 (6: 7: 6: 7: 7) sts at beg of foll alt row.

Work 1 row straight.

Cast off rem 6 (6: 6: 7: 7: 8) sts.

Left front

Using 4mm needles, cast on 36 (38: 40: 42: 44: 46) sts.

K 4 rows.

Change to 4.5mm needles and cont in st st with rib borders as foll:

Next row (RS): P1, k1, p1, m1, k to last 3 sts, p1, k1, p1.

Next row: K1, p1, k1, p to last 3 sts, k1, p1, k1.

Rep last 2 rows 3 times more.

40 (42: 44: 46: 48: 50) sts.

This completes side-slit border. now completed.

Cont in st st throughout and keeping 3 rib sts as set along centre front only (end of RS rows and beg of WS rows), dec 1 st at side edge only on 7th row and every foll 7th (8th: 8th: 8th: 9th: 9th) row until 37 (39: 41: 43: 45: 47) sts rem.

Work 15 (17: 17: 19: 19: 19) rows straight, ending with RS facing for next row.

Inc 1 st at side edge on next row and every foll 7th (8th: 8th: 9th: 9th: 9th) row until there are 40 (42: 44: 46: 48: 50) sts.

Cont straight until front measures 29 (29: 29: 28.5: 28: 28)cm from cast-on edge, ending with RS facing for next row.

Shape armhole

Cast off 4 (4: 4: 5: 5: 5) sts at beg of row.

36 (38: 40: 41: 43: 45) sts.

Dec 1 st at armhole edge of next 3 rows, then on foll 2 alt rows.

31 (33: 35: 36: 38: 40) sts.

Cont straight until armhole measures 11 (11: 12.5: 14: 14.5: 15)cm, ending at centre front edge.

Shape neck

Cast off 6 (6: 7: 7: 8: 8) sts at beg of next row.

25 (27: 28: 29: 30: 32) sts.

Dec 1 st at neck edge of next 7 rows, then on foll 2 (2: 2: 3: 3: 3) alt rows.

16 (18: 19: 19: 20: 22) sts.

Cont straight until armhole matches back to shoulder shaping, ending at armhole edge.

Shape shoulder

Cast off 5 (6: 6: 6: 6: 7) sts at beg of next row and 5 (6: 7: 6: 7: 7) sts at beg of foll alt row.

Work 1 row straight.

Cast off rem 6 (6: 6: 7: 7: 8) sts.

Sleeves (make 2)

To make cuff slit, use 2 balls of yarn to cast on as foll:

Using 4mm needles, cast on 21 (22: 22: 23: 23: 24) sts with one ball and 21 (22: 22: 23: 23: 24) sts with 2nd ball onto same needle.

Working both sides of slit separately but at same time, k 4 rows.

Change to 4.5mm needles.

Next row (RS): K to last 3 sts, p1, k1, p1 on first piece; then on 2nd piece, p1, k1, p1, k to end of row.

Next row: Rib sts as set and p rem sts.

Rep last 2 rows once more.

Next row (inc row) (RS): K to last 3 sts, m1, p1, k1, p1 on first piece; then on 2nd piece, p1, k1, p1, m1, k to end.

Cont in rib and st st as set, inc 1 st on each piece as before on foll 6th row. *23 (24: 24: 25: 25: 26) sts on each piece.*

Work 1 row straight as set on both pieces, ending with RS facing for next row.

To join pieces, k across all sts using the first ball of yarn. *46 (48: 48: 50: 50: 52) sts.*

Break off 2nd ball of yarn.

P 1 row.

Cont in st st throughout, inc 1 st at each end of next row and every foll 12th row until there are 60 (62: 62: 64: 64: 66) sts.

Cont straight until sleeve measures 38 (39.5: 39.5: 39.5: 42: 42)cm from cast-on edge, ending with RS facing for next row.

Shape top

Cast off 4 (4: 4: 5: 5: 5) sts at beg of next 2 rows. *52 (54: 54: 54: 54: 56) sts.*

Dec 1 st each end of next 4 rows, then on foll 2 alt rows, then every 4th row until 34 (34: 32: 32: 30: 30) sts rem.

P 1 row.

Dec 1 st at each end of next and every foll alt row until 26 (28: 28: 28: 28: 28) sts rem, then on foll 3 rows. *20 (22: 22: 22: 22: 22) sts.*

Cast off 3 sts at beg of next 4 rows. *8 (10: 10: 10: 10: 10) sts.*

Cast off rem 8 (10: 10: 10: 10: 10) sts.

Small pockets (make 2)

Using 4.5mm needles, cast on 11 (11: 11: 13: 13: 13) sts.

***Row 1 (RS):** P1, k1, p1, k to last 3 sts, p1, k1, p1.

Row 2: K1, p1, k1, p to last 3 sts, k1, p1, k1.

Row 3: P1, k1, p1, m1, k to last 3 sts, m1, p1, k1, p1.

Row 4: Rep row 2.***

Rep last 2 rows until there are 17 (17: 17: 19: 19: 19) sts.

Keeping 3 rib sts as set at each side and working rem sts in st st, cont straight until pocket measures 7.5 (7.5: 7.5: 9: 9: 9)cm, ending WS facing for next row.

Change to 4mm needles and k 3 rows.

Cast off knitwise.

Large pockets (make 2)

Using 4.5mm needles, cast on 15 (15: 15: 17: 17: 17) sts.

Work as for small pockets from *** to ***.

Rep last 2 rows until there are 21 (21: 21: 23: 23: 23) sts.

Keeping 3 rib sts as set at each side and working rem sts in st st, cont straight until pocket measures 9 (9: 9: 10: 10: 10)cm, ending with WS facing for next row.

Change to 4mm needles and k 3 rows.

Cast off knitwise.

To finish

Weave in any loose yarn ends.

Gently press and steam.

Sew shoulder seams.

Sew sleeve heads to armholes.

Sew side seams and sleeve seams, leaving slits open.

Sew on pockets.

Sew ribbons (with one colour slightly overlapping the other as shown in photograph) to tops of large pockets, along both fronts and neckline, and around cuff edge, taking particular care to trace around cuff slits.

Sew top of each cuff slit together with a little stitch.

slouch socks

materials

Any medium-weight wool yarn, such as Rowan *RYC Cashsoft Aran*
or Debbie Bliss *Cashmerino Aran*
3 (4) x 50g balls
Pair each of 4.5mm and 5mm knitting needles

size

One size, to fit woman's average-size foot (the length of the foot
can be lengthed or shortened by working more or fewer rows
where indicated)

tension

19 sts and 25 rows to 10cm over st st using 4.5mm needles
18 sts and 24 rows to 10cm over st st using 5mm needles

pattern note

• Knit the long socks shown in the photograph, or follow the
alternative instructions for the short socks.

slouch socks

Short socks

Right sock
Using 5mm needles, cast on 40 sts.
Work 6.5cm in k1, p1 rib.
Change to 4.5mm needles and cont
in rib as set until rib measures
12.5cm.
Beg with a k row, work in st st until
sock measures 19.5cm from cast-on
edge, ending with RS facing for
next row.

Shape heel
Next row (RS): K2, k2tog, k12,
k2tog tbl, k2, then turn, leaving rem
20 sts on a holder.
Next row: P.
Next row: K2, k2tog, k to last 4 sts,
k2tog tbl, k2.
Next row: P.
Rep last 2 rows until 8 sts rem.
Next row (RS): K2, m1, k to last
2 sts, m1, k2.
Next row: P.
Rep last 2 rows until there are 20 sts
on needle.
Next row: K 20 sts on needle, then
k 20 sts from holder. *40 sts.*
Work 12.5cm straight, ending with
RS facing for next row.
Note: Adjust length of sock here
by working more or fewer rows
straight.

Shape toe
Next row (RS): K2, k2tog, k12,
k2tog tbl, k2, then turn, leaving rem
20 sts on a holder.
Next row: P.
Next row: K2, k2tog, k to last 4 sts,
k2tog tbl, k2.
Next row: P.
Rep last 2 rows once more. *14 sts.*
Dec 1 st at each end of next 3 rows
as set. *8 sts.*
P 1 row.
Cast off.
With RS facing, rejoin yarn to rem
20 sts on holder and complete to
match first side.

Left sock
Using 5mm needles, cast on 40 sts
and work 6.5cm in k1, p1 rib.
Change to 4.5mm needles and cont
in rib as set until rib measures
12.5cm.
Beg with a k row, work in st st until
sock measures 19.5cm from cast-on
edge, ending with WS facing for
next row.
Next row: P20, then turn, leaving
rem sts on a holder.

Shape heel
Next row: K2, k2tog, k12, k2tog
tbl, k2.
Next row: P.

Next row: K2, k2tog, k to last 4 sts,
k2tog tbl, k2.
Next row: P.
Rep last 2 rows until 8 sts rem.
Next row (RS): K2, m1, k to last
2 sts, m1, k2.
Next row: P.
Next row: K2, m1, k to last 2 sts,
m1, k2.
Rep last 2 rows until there are 20 sts
on needle.
Next row: P 20 sts on needle, then
p 20 sts from holder. *40 sts.*
Work 12.5cm straight, ending with
RS facing for next row.
Note: Adjust length of sock here
by working more or fewer rows
straight.

Shape toe
Next row (RS): K2, k2tog, k12,
k2tog tbl, k2, then turn, leaving rem
20 sts on a holder.
Next row: P.
Next row: K2, k2tog, k to last
4 sts, k2tog tbl, k2.
Next row: P.
Rep last 2 rows once more. *14 sts.*
Dec 1 st at each end of next 3 rows
as set. *8 sts.*
P 1 row. Cast off.
With RS facing, rejoin yarn to rem
20 sts on holder and complete to
match first side.

Long socks

Right sock

Using 5mm needles, cast on 46 sts.
Work 12.5cm in k1, p1 rib.
Change to 4.5mm needles and beg
with a k row, work in st st, dec 1 st
each end of 19th row and every foll
20th row until 40 sts rem.
Cont straight until sock measures
38cm from cast-on edge, ending
with RS facing for next row.

Shape heel

Next row: K2, k2tog, k12, k2tog
tbl, k2, then turn, leaving rem 20 sts
on a holder.
Next row: P.
Next row: K2, k2tog, k to last
4 sts, k2tog tbl, k2.
Next row: P.
Rep last 2 rows until 8 sts rem.
Next row (RS): K2, m1, k to last
2 sts, m1, k2.
Next row: P.
Rep last 2 rows until there are 20
sts on needle.
Next row (RS): K 20 sts on
needle, then k 20 sts from holder.
40 sts.
Work 12.5cm straight, ending with
RS facing for next row.
Note: *Adjust length of sock here
by working more or fewer rows
straight.*

Shape toe

Next row: K2, k2tog, k12, k2tog
tbl, k2, then turn, leaving rem 20 sts
on a holder.
Next row: P.
Next row: K2, k2tog, k to last
4 sts, k2tog tbl, k2.
Next row: P.
Rep last 2 rows once more. *14 sts.*
Dec 1 st at each end of next 3 rows
as set. *8 sts.*
P 1 row.
Cast off.
With RS facing, rejoin yarn to rem
20 sts on holder and complete to
match first side.

Left sock

Using 5mm needles, cast on 46 sts.
Work 12.5cm in k1, p1 rib.
Change to 4.5mm needles and beg
with a k row, work in st st, dec 1 st
at each end of 19th row and every
foll 20th row until 40 sts rem.
Cont straight until sock measures
38cm from cast-on edge, ending
with WS facing for next row.
Next row (WS): P20, then turn,
leaving rem sts on a holder.

Shape heel

Next row: K2, k2tog, k12, k2tog
tbl, k 2.
Next row: P.
Next row: K2, k2tog, k to last 4 sts,
k2tog tbl, k2.
Next row: P.
Rep last 2 rows until 8 sts rem.
Next row (RS): K2, m1, k to last
2 sts, m1, k2.
Next row: P.

Next row: K2, m1, k to last 2 sts,
m1, k2.
Rep last 2 rows until there are 20
sts on needle.
Next row: P 20 sts on needle, then
p 20 sts from holder. *40 sts.*
Work 12.5cm straight, ending with
RS facing for next row.
Note: *Adjust length of sock here
by working more or fewer rows
straight.*

Shape toe

Next row: K2, k2tog, k12, k2tog
tbl, k2, then turn, leaving rem 20
sts on a holder.
Next row: P.
Next row: K2, k2tog, k to last 4 sts,
k2tog tbl, k 2.
Next row: P.
Rep last 2 rows once more. *14 sts.*
Dec 1 st at each end of next 3 rows
as set. *8 sts.*
P 1 row.
Cast off.
With RS facing, rejoin yarn to rem
20 sts on holder and complete to
match first side.

To finish

Weave in any loose yarn ends.
Lay work out flat and gently steam
to enhance yarn.
Sew two heel seams first.
Sew side seam, starting at toe with
an invisible seam and reversing
seam on turnover part of rib.

camisole

materials

Any fine-weight 4ply mercerized cotton yarn, such as Yeoman's
Cotton Cannele 4ply
2 x 250g cones or 1275 (1360: 1445: 1530: 1615: 1700)m
Pair each of 3mm and 3.25mm knitting needles
Cable needle

sizes

dress size	8	10	12	14	16	18	
to fit bust	81	86	91	97	102	107	cm
actual bust	81	86	91	97	102	107	cm
length	46	48	51	53	56	58.5	cm

tension

29 sts and 36 rows to 10cm over st st using 3.25mm needles·

camisole

stitches

decreasing with an eyelet
K3, k2tog, yfwd, k2tog, k to last 7 sts, k2tog tbl, yfwd, k2tog tbl, k3.
increasing with an eyelet
K3, yfwd, k to last 3 sts, yfwd, k3.
C4F (cable 4 front)
Slip next 2 sts onto cn and leave at front of work, k2, then k2 from cn.

Back
Using 3mm needles, cast on 108
(114: 120: 126: 132: 138) sts.
Work 2cm in k1, p1 rib.
Change to 3.25mm needles and
beg with a k row, work in st st,
dec 1 st with an eyelet at each end
of 5th row and every foll 6th row
until 100 (106: 112: 118: 124: 130)
sts rem.
Work 19 (19: 21: 21: 23: 23) rows
straight, ending with RS facing for
next row.
Cont in st st throughout, inc 1 st
with an eyelet at each end of next
row and every foll 6th (6th: 6th:
8th: 8th: 8th) row until there are
116 (122: 128: 134: 140: 146) sts.

Cont straight until back measures
25.5 (26.5: 28.5: 30: 30.5: 32)cm
from cast-on edge, ending with RS
facing for next row.
Divide for neck
**Working each side separately,
divide for neck as foll:
Next row (RS): K55 (58: 61: 64:
67: 70), p1, k1, p1, then turn,
leaving rem 58 (61: 64: 67: 70: 73)
sts on a holder.
Next row: K1, p1, k1, p to end.
Next row (dec row): K to last 5
sts, k2tog tbl, p1, k1, p1.
***Keeping neck rib border as set,
cont to dec 1 st as set at neck edge
on every alt row **and at the same
time** when back measures 28 (29:

31: 32.5: 33: 34.5)cm from cast-on
edge, ending with RS facing, shape
armhole as foll:
Shape armhole
Cast off 5 sts at beg of next row.
Work 1 row straight.
Dec 1 st at armhole edge on next
9 rows, then on foll 7 alt rows, using
an eyelet decrease on first of these
decreases and every foll 4th row.
Cont dec as set at neck edge only
on alt rows until 10 (10: 10: 10: 12:
12) sts rem.
Cont straight, ribbing across all sts
as set, until armhole measures 18
(19: 20: 21.5: 23: 24)cm.
Cast off in rib.
With RS facing. rejoin yarn to sts

on holder and cont as foll:
Next row: P1, k1, p1, k to end
of row.
Next row: P to last 3 sts, k1, p1, k1.
Next row (dec row): P1, k1, p1,
k2tog, k to end.
Complete to match first side from
***, reversing all shaping.

Front
Work as for back **and at the same
time** 24 rows before start of neck
shaping, place a marker at centre of
sts and cont with side increases as
set, work as foll:
Row 1: K to 3 sts before marker,
p1, C4F, p1, k to end.
Row 2: P to 3 sts before marker,

k1, p4, k1, p to end.
Row 3: K to 3 sts before marker,
p1, k4, p1, k to end.
Row 4: Rep row 2.
Rep rows 1–4 once more, then rows
1 and 2 again.
Row 11: K.
Row 12: P.
Row 13: K to marker, yon, k to end.
Row 14: P, move marker to
centre st.
Row 15: K.
Row 16: P.
Row 17: K to marker, p1, k to end.
Row 18: P to 1 st before marker,
k1, p1, k1, p to end.
Row 19: K to 2 sts before marker,
[p1, k1] twice, p1, k to end.

Row 20: P to 1 st before marker,
k1, p1, k1, p to end.
Row 21: K to marker, p1, k to end.
Row 22: P.
Row 23: K.
Row 24: P58 (61: 64: 67: 70: 73),
p2tog, p to end of row.
116 (122: 128: 134: 140: 146) sts.
Complete as for back from **.

To finish
Weave in any loose yarn ends.
Gently steam and press pieces
under a damp cloth.
Sew shoulder seams with a flat seam.
Sew side seams.

silk shrug

materials

Any lightweight silk yarn, such as Jaeger *Silk DK*
  6 (6: 6: 7: 7: 8) x 50g balls
Pair each of 3.25mm and 3.75mm knitting needles
3.25mm circular knitting needle

sizes

dress size	8	10	12	14	16	18	
to fit bust	81	86	91	97	102	107	cm
actual bust	85	88	92	95	98	102	cm
length	33	35.5	37	38	39	41	cm

tension

24 sts and 34 rows to 10cm over st st using 3.75mm needles

pattern note

• To create a fully fashioned detail, work increases and decreases three stitches inside the edges. Work the decreases through the back of loops as foll:
On a k row: K3, k2tog, k to last 5 sts, k2tog tbl, k3.
On a p row: P3, p2tog tbl, p to last 5 sts, p2tog, p3.

silk shrug

Back
Using 3.25mm needles, cast on
90 (94: 98: 102: 106: 110) sts.
Work 3.5cm in k1, p1 rib.
Change to 3.75mm needles and
beg with a k row, work in st st, inc
1 st at each end of 9th row and
every foll 6th row until there are
102 (106: 110: 114: 118: 122) sts.
Cont in st st throughout, work
9 (13: 13: 15: 17: 17) rows straight.
Shape armhole
Cast off 4 (4: 5: 5: 6: 6) sts at beg of
next 2 rows.
Dec 1 st at each end of next 9 rows.
76 (80: 82: 86: 88: 92) sts.
Work 45 (49: 53: 57: 57: 61) rows
straight.
Shape shoulders
Cast off 12 (13: 13: 13: 13: 14) sts at
beg of next 2 rows and 13 (13: 13:
14: 14: 14) sts at beg of foll 2 rows.
Cast off rem 26 (28: 30: 32: 34: 36) sts.

Right front
Using 3.75mm needles, cast on 7 (9:
11: 13: 15: 17) sts.
Row 1 (RS): K.
Row 2: P to last 3 sts, p into front
and back of next st, p2.
Row 3: K1, k into front and back
of next st, k to end.
Rows 4–7: Rep rows 2 and 3 twice.
Row 8: Rep row 2.
Row 9: K1, k into front and back
of next st, k to last 3 sts, k into front
and back of next st, k2.
Row 10: Rep row 2.
Row 11: Rep row 3.
Row 12: Rep row 2.
Row 13: Rep row 3.
Row 14: Rep row 2.
Rep rows 9–14 twice.
Rep rows 9–11 once.
Cont in st st throughout, work 20 (24:
24: 26: 28: 28) rows, inc 1 st at end of
4th and 10th rows as set, ending with

WS facing for next row.
41 (43: 45: 47: 49: 51) sts.
Shape armhole
**Cast off 5 (6: 7: 8: 8: 8) sts at beg
of next row.
Dec 1 st at armhole edge on next
11 (11: 12: 12: 15: 15) rows.
25 (26: 26: 27: 27: 28) sts.
Cont straight until armhole
matches back to shoulder shaping,
ending with WS facing for next row.
Shape shoulder
Cast off 12 (13: 13: 13: 14: 14) sts
at beg of next row.
Work 1 row.
Cast off rem 13 (13: 13: 14: 14: 14)
sts.**

Left front
Using 3.75mm needles, cast on 7 (9:
11: 13: 15: 17) sts.
Row 1 (RS): K.
Row 2: P1, p into front and back

of next st, p to end.
Row 3: K to last 3 sts, k into front and back of next st, k2.
Rows 4–7: Rep rows 2 and 3 twice.
Row 8: Rep row 2.
Row 9: K1, k into front and back of next st, k to last 3 sts, k into front and back of next st, k2.
Row 10: Rep row 2.
Row 11: Rep row 3.
Row 12: Rep row 2.
Row 13: Rep row 3.
Row 14: Rep row 2.
Rep rows 9–14 twice.
Rep rows 9–11 once.
Cont in st st throughout, work 19 (23: 23: 25: 27: 27) rows, inc 1 st at beg of 4th and 10th rows as set, ending with RS facing for next row.
41 (43: 45: 47: 49: 51) sts.
Complete as for right front from ** to **.
Sleeves

Using 3.25mm needles, cast on 72 (76: 80: 84: 88: 92) sts.
Work 3.5cm in k1, p1 rib.
Change to 3.75mm needles and beg with a k row, work in st st, shaping sleeve top as foll:
Dec 1 st each end of next 5 rows.
62 (66: 70: 74: 78: 82) sts.
Dec 1 st at each end of every foll alt row until 28 (30: 32: 34: 36: 38) sts rem.
Work 1 row.
Dec 1 st at each end of next 4 rows.
Cast off 3 sts at beg of next 4 rows.
Cast off rem 8 (10: 12: 14: 16: 18) sts.

To finish
Weave in any loose yarn ends.
Lay work out flat and gently steam.
Sew both shoulder seams.
Front bands
Using 3.25mm circular needle and with RS of right front facing, rejoin

yarn at side edge and pick up and k 112 (118: 124: 130: 136: 142) sts up right front, 26 (28: 30: 32: 34: 36) sts across back neck, and 112 (118: 124: 130: 136: 142) sts down left front.
250 (264: 278: 292: 306: 320) sts.
Working in rows rather than rounds, work 3.5cm in k1, p1 rib.
Cast off in rib.

To finish
Sew sleeve heads into armholes with an invisible seam.
Join side seams with an invisible seam.

gloves

materials

Any double-knitting-weight cotton-blend yarn, such as Rowan
   RYC Cashcotton DK
   2 x 50g balls
Pair each of 3mm and 3.25mm knitting needles

size

One size, to fit worman's average-size hand

tension

25 sts and 34 rows to 10cm over st st using 3.25mm needles

pattern note

• As an alternative, instructions are given for fingerless gloves
  as well.

gloves

Gloves

Right glove
Using 3mm needles, cast on 44 sts.
Work 8cm in k1, p1 rib.
Change to 3.25mm needles and
beg with a k row, work 8 rows in
st st.
Shape thumb
Row 1 (RS): K21, p1, k into front
and back of next st, k1, k into front
and back of next st, p1, k18. *46 sts.*
Row 2: P18, k1, p5, k1, p21.
Row 3: K21, p1, k5, p1, k18.
Row 4: Rep row 2.
Row 5: K21, p1, k into front and
back of next st, k3, k into front and
back of next st, p1, k18. *48 sts.*
Cont to inc 1 st at each side of
thumb gusset on every 4th row until
there are 56 sts, keeping p st at
either side to define shaping.
Work 1 row straight.
Next row: K37, turn, cast on 2 sts.
Next row: P16, turn, cast on 2 sts.
18 sts.
**Work 16 rows on these 18 sts.
Next row: K1, [k2, k2tog] 4 times,
k1.
Next row: P.
Next row: [K2tog] 5 times, k4.
9 sts.
Break off yarn leaving a long end,

thread through rem sts, gather
tightly, secure firmly, then sew
thumb seam.
With right-hand needle, rejoin yarn
and pick up and k 4 sts at base of
thumb, then k to end of row. *46 sts.*
Work 11 rows.
Shape first finger
Next row: K29, turn, cast on 1 st.
Next row: P13, turn, cast on 1 st.
14 sts.
Work 22 rows on these 14 sts.
Next row: K1, [k2, k2tog] 3 times, k1.
Next row: P.
Next row: K2, [k2tog] 4 times, k1.
7 sts.
Break off yarn leaving a long end,
thread through rem sts, gather
tightly, secure firmly, then sew
finger seam.
Shape second finger
With right-hand needle, rejoin
yarn and pick up and k 2 sts at
base of first finger, then k6, turn,
cast on 1 st.
Next row: P15, turn, cast on 1 st.
16 sts.
Work 26 rows.
Next row: K2, [k2tog, k2] 3 times, k2.
Next row: P.
Next row: K1, [k2tog] 6 times.
7 sts.
Complete as for first finger.

Shape third finger
With right-hand needle, rejoin
yarn and pick up and k 2 sts at
base of second finger, then k6, turn,
cast on 1 st.
Next row: P15, turn, cast on 1 st.
16 sts.
Work 22 rows.
Complete as for second finger.
Shape fourth finger
With right-hand needle, rejoin yarn
and pick up and k 2 sts at base of
third finger, then k5. *12 sts.*
Work 19 rows.
Next row: K2, [k2, k2tog] twice, k2.
Next row: P.
Next row: [K2tog] 5 times. *5 sts.*
Complete as for second finger and
sew down side seam to wrist.**

Left glove
Work to match right glove, reversing
position of thumb gusset by
shaping as foll:
Row 1 (RS): K18, p1, k into front
and back of next st, k1, k into front
and back of next st, p1, k21. 46 sts.
Row 2: P21, k1, p5, k1, p18.
Row 3: K18, p1, k5, p1, k21.
Row 4: Rep row 2.
Row 5: K18, p1, k into front and
back of next st, k3, k into front and
back of next st, p1, k21. *48 sts.*

Cont to inc 1 st at each side of thumb gusset on every 4th row until there are 56 sts, keeping p st at either side to define shaping.
Work 1 row straight.
Next row: K34, turn, cast on 2 sts.
Next row: P16, turn, cast on 2 sts. *18 sts.*
Complete as for right glove, working from ** to **.

To finish
Steam gloves to enhance the yarn. Sew side seam and finger seams with mattress st for invisible finish.

Fingerless gloves

Right glove
Using 3mm needles, cast on 44 sts.
Work 5.5cm in k1, p1 rib.
Change to 3.25mm needles and cont in rib as set until work measures 14cm from cast-on edge, ending with RS facing for next row.
Shape thumb gussett
Row 1 (RS): K21, p1, k into front and back of next st, k1, k into front and back of next st, p1, k18. *46 sts.*
Row 2: P18, k1, p5, k1, p21.
Row 3: K21, p1, k5, p1, k18.
Row 4: Rep row 2.
Row 5: K21, p1, k into front and back of next st, k3, k into front and back of next st, p1, k18. *48 sts.*
Cont to inc 1 st each side of thumb gusset on every 4th row until there are 56 sts, keeping p st at either side to define shaping.
Work 1 row straight.
Next row: K37, turn, cast on 2 sts.
Next row: P16, turn, cast on 2 sts. *18 sts.*
***Work 4 rows st st, then 4 rows of k1, p1 rib on these 18 sts.
Cast off in rib.
Break off yarn leaving a long end and sew thumb seam.
With right-hand needle, rejoin yarn and pick up and k 4 sts at base of thumb, then k to end of row. *46 sts.*
Work 9 rows in st st.
Work 4 rows in k1, p1 rib.
Cast off in rib.
Break off yarn leaving a long end to sew side seam.***

Left glove
Work to match right glove, reversing position of thumb gusset as foll:
Row 1 (RS): K18, p1, k into front and back of next st, k1, k into front and back of next st, p1, k21. *46 sts.*
Row 2: P21, k1, p5, k1, p18.
Row 3: K18, p1, k5, p1, k21.

Row 4: Rep row 2.
Row 5: K18, p1, k into front and back of next st, k3, k into front and back of next st, p1, k21. *48 sts.*
Cont to inc 1 st at each side of thumb gusset on every 4th row until there are 56 sts, keeping p st at either side to define shaping.
Work 1 row straight.
Next row: K34, turn, cast on 2 sts.
Next row: P16, turn, cast on 2 sts. *18 sts.*
Complete as for right glove, working from *** to ***.

To finish
Steam gloves to enhance the yarn. Sew the side seam with mattress st for invisible finish.

deep-v sweater

materials

Any lightweight cotton-blend yarn, such as Debbie Bliss *Cathay*
10 (11: 11: 12: 12: 13) x 50g balls
Pair each of 3mm and 3.75mm knitting needles

sizes

dress size	8	10	12	14	16	18	
to fit bust	81	86	91	97	102	107	cm
actual bust	86	92	97	103	108	114	cm
length	56	58	58	61	61	63.5	cm
sleeve seam	44.5	46	46	47	47	48	cm

tension

22 sts and 30 rows to 10cm over st st using 3.75mm needles

pattern notes

• To create a fully fashioned detail, work increases and decreases
  three stitches inside the edges. Work decreases through the back of
  loops as foll:
  On a k row: K3, k2tog, k to last 5 sts, k2tog tbl, k3.
  On a p row: P3, p2tog tbl, p to last 5 sts, p2tog, p3.
• When picking up sts around the neck, pick up and knit one stitch
  for every stitch and 3 stitches for every 4 rows.

deep-v sweater

Back

Using 3mm needles, cast on 96 (102: 108: 114: 120: 126) sts.
Work 7cm in k1, p1 rib.
Change to 3.75mm needles and beg with a k row, work in st st, dec 1 st at each end of 9th (11th: 11th: 13th: 13th: 15th) row and every foll 12th row until 90 (96: 102: 108: 114: 120) sts rem.
Cont in st st throughout, work 19 (21: 21: 23: 23: 25) rows straight, ending with RS facing for next row.
Inc 1 st at each end of next row and every foll 12th row until there are 96 (102: 108: 114: 120: 126) sts.
Cont straight until back measures 38 (39: 38: 40: 39: 40.5)cm from cast-on edge, ending with RS facing for next row.

Shape armhole

Cast off 5 sts at beg of next 2 rows.
86 (92: 98: 104: 110: 116) sts.
Dec 1 st at each end of next 5 rows.
76 (82: 88: 94: 100: 106) sts.
Dec 1 st at each end of next 3 alt rows.
70 (76: 82: 88: 94: 100) sts.
Cont straight until armhole measures 18 (19: 20: 21: 22: 23)cm, ending with RS facing for next row.

Shape shoulders and neck

Next row (RS): Cast off 8 (9: 10: 11: 12: 13) sts, k until there are 13 (14: 15: 17: 18: 19) sts on right-hand needle, then turn, leaving rem sts on a holder.
Cast off 4 (4: 4: 5: 5: 5) sts at beg of next row.
Cast off rem 9 (10: 11: 12: 13: 14) sts.
With RS of work facing, rejoin yarn to rem sts and cast off 28 (30: 32: 32: 34: 36) sts, then k to end.
Complete to match first side, reversing all shaping.

Front

Work as for back, but when work measures 22.5 (23.5: 23.5: 24.5: 24.5: 25)cm from cast-on edge, ending with RS facing for next row, divide for neck as foll:
Count sts on needle to find centre of front and mark centre.
Next row: K to centre, then turn, leaving rem sts on a holder.
Work side and armhole shaping as for back **and at the same time** working each side of neck separately, shape neck as foll:
P 1 row.
Next row: K to last 5 sts, k2tog tbl, k3.
Dec 1 st at neck edge on every foll 4th row 13 times more, then on every foll 6th row 5 times.
17 (19: 21: 23: 25: 27) sts.
Work straight until front matches back to shoulder shaping, ending with RS facing for next row.

Shape shoulders

Cast off 8 (9: 10: 11: 12: 13) sts, work to end of row.

P 1 row.

Cast off rem 9 (10: 11: 12: 13: 14) sts.
With RS facing, rejoin yarn to rem
sts and k to end.

P 1 row.

Next row: K3, k2tog, k to end.
Complete to match first side,
reversing all shaping.

Sleeves (make 2)

Using 3mm needles, cast on
60 (60: 62: 62: 64: 64) sts.
Work 7cm in k1, p1 rib.
Change to 3.75mm needles and
beg with a k row, work in st st, inc
1 st at each end of 11th row and
every foll 12th row until there aer
76 (76: 78: 78: 80: 80) sts.
Cont straight until sleeve measures
44.5 (46: 46: 47: 47: 48)cm from
cast-on edge, ending with RS facing
for next row.

Shape top

Cast off 5 sts at beg of next 2 rows.

66 (66: 68: 68: 70: 70) sts.
Dec 1 st at each end of next
5 rows, then on every foll alt row
until 24 sts rem.
Dec 1 st at each end of next 5 rows.
Cast off rem 14 sts.

To finish

Weave in any loose yarn ends.
Gently steam to enhance the yarn.
Sew right shoulder seam.

Neckband

Using 3mm needles and with RS
facing, pick up and k 75 (77: 77: 81:
81: 85) sts down left side of neck,
place a marker on needle, pick up
and k 75 (77: 77: 81: 81: 85) sts up
right side of neck, and 36 (38: 38:
42: 44: 46) sts across back neck.
186 (192: 192: 204: 206: 216) sts.
Work in k1, p1 rib as foll:
Row 1 (WS): Beg with k1, work in
k1, p1 rib over first 111 (115: 115:
123: 125: 131) sts (ending with k1),

slip marker to right-hand needle,
beg with k1, work in k1, p1 rib
to end.
Row 2: Rib as set to 2 sts before
marker, k2tog tbl, slip marker to
right-hand needle, k2tog, rib to end.
Row 3: Rib as set to 2 sts before
marker, p2tog, slip marker to right-
hand needle, p2tog tbl, rib to end.
Rep last 2 rows until neckband
measures 2.5cm.
Cast off in rib.
Sew left shoulder seam.
Sew sleeve heads to armholes with
an invisible seam.
Sew side and sleeve seams with an
invisible seam.

classic roll neck

materials

Any double-knitting-weight wool yarn, such as Rowan
  RYC Cashsoft DK
  9 (9: 10: 10: 11: 11) x 50g balls
Pair each of 3.75mm and 4mm knitting needles
3.75mm circular knitting needle, for collar

sizes

dress size	8	10	12	14	16	18	
to fit bust	81	86	91	97	102	107	cm
actual bust	86	92	97	103	108	114	cm
length	56	58	58	61	61	63.5	cm
sleeve seam	44.5	46	46	47	47	48	cm

tension

22 sts and 30 rows to 10cm over st st using 4mm needles

pattern notes

• When making a folded, knitted-on hem, cast on with a size larger
  needle (i.e., use 4mm) as it makes it easier to see the sts when
  joining loops for the hem. When working the turning row for hem,
  use a size smaller needle (i.e., use 3.25mm) for a neater finish.
• To create a fully fashioned detail, work increases and decreases
  three stitches inside the edges. Work the decreases through the
  back of loops as foll:
  On a k row: K3, k2tog, k to last 5 sts, k2tog tbl, k3.
  On a p row: P3, p2tog tbl, p to last 5 sts, p2tog, p3.

classic roll neck

Back
With 3.75mm needles, cast on 64
(70: 76: 82: 88: 94) sts.
Work 6cm in st st, ending with RS
facing for next row.
Next row (RS): P (to make fold
line for hem).
Change to 4mm needles and beg
with p row, work 6cm in st st,
ending with RS facing for next row.
Next row (RS): To make hem,
k tog 1 st from needle and 1 loop
from cast-on edge all across row.
Next row: P.**
Next row: K0 (3: 6: 9: 12: 15),
*k into front and back of next st,
k1, rep from * to last 0 (3: 6: 9: 12:
15) sts, k 0 (3: 6: 9: 12: 15).
96 (102: 108: 114: 120: 126) sts.
Cont in st st throughout, work until
back measures 38 (39: 38: 40: 39:
40.5)cm from hem fold line row,

ending with RS facing for next row.
Shape armholes
Cast off 5 sts at beg of next 2 rows.
86 (92: 98: 104: 110: 116) sts.
Dec 1 st at each end of next 5 rows.
76 (82: 88: 94: 100: 106) sts.
Dec 1 st at each end of next 3 alt rows.
70 (76: 82: 88: 94: 100) sts.
Cont straight until armhole
measures 18 (19: 20: 21: 22: 23)cm,
ending with RS facing for next row.
Shape shoulders and neck
Next row (RS): Cast off 8 (9: 10:
11: 12: 13) sts, k until there are 13
(14: 16: 17: 18: 19) sts on right-
hand needle, then turn, leaving rem
sts on a holder.
Cast off 4 (4: 5: 5: 5: 5) sts at beg of
next row.
Cast off rem 9 (10: 11: 12: 13: 14) sts.
With RS facing, slip centre 28 (30:
30: 32: 34: 36) sts onto a holder,

then rejoin yarn to rem sts and
complete to match first side,
reversing all shaping.

Front
Work as for back until 12 (12:
14: 14: 14: 16) rows fewer have
been worked to start of shoulder
shaping, ending with RS facing
for next row.
Shape neck
Next row: K25 (27: 30: 32: 34:
37), then turn, leaving rem sts on
a holder.
Cast off 4 (4: 4: 5: 5: 5) sts at beg
of next row.
21 (23: 26: 27: 29: 32) sts.
Dec 1 st at neck edge on next
3 rows, then on foll alt rows until
17 (19: 21: 23: 25: 27) sts rem.
Work 5 rows straight, ending with
RS facing for next row.

Shape shoulder

Cast off 8 (9: 10: 11: 12: 13) sts at beg of next row.

Work 1 row.

Cast off rem 9 (10: 11: 12: 13: 14) sts.

With RS facing, slip centre 20 (22: 22: 24: 26: 26) sts onto a holder and rejoin yarn to rem sts, then k to end.

Complete to match first side, reversing all shaping and working 1 extra row before start of shoulder shaping.

Sleeves (make 2)

Using 3.75mm needles, cast on 35 (38: 41: 44: 47: 50) sts.

Work hem as for back to **.

Next row (RS): K into front and back of every st across row.

70 (76: 82: 88: 94: 100) sts.

Cont in st st throughout, work until sleeve measures 44.5 (46: 46: 47: 47: 48)cm from hem fold line row, ending with RS facing for next row.

Shape top

Cast off 5 sts at beg of next 2 rows.

60 (66: 72: 78: 84: 90) sts.

Dec 1 st at each end of next 5 rows.

50 (56: 62: 68: 74: 80) sts.

Dec 1 st at each end of every foll alt row until 20 (24: 26: 32: 36: 40) sts rem, then at each end of next 3 (5: 5: 7: 7: 9) rows.

Cast off rem 14 (14: 16: 18: 22: 22) sts.

To finish

Weave in any loose yarn ends.

Sew shoulder seams.

Collar

Using 3.75mm circular needle and with RS facing, pick up and k 16 (16: 19: 19: 19: 20) sts down left front neck, 20 (22: 22: 24: 26: 26) sts from holder, 16 (16: 19: 19: 19: 20) sts up right front neck, 4 (4: 5: 5: 5: 5) sts down right back neck, 28 (30: 30: 32: 34: 36) sts from holder, and 4 (4: 5: 5: 5: 5) sts up left back neck.

88 (92: 100: 104: 108: 112) sts.

Work in k2, p2 rib for 9cm.

Change to 4mm needles and work 9cm more as set.

Cast off in rib.

Weave in any loose yarn ends.

Lay work out flat and steam gently to enhance yarn.

Sew sleeve seams and cuffs with an invisible seam.

Sew side and hem seams with an invisible seam.

Set in sleeves and sew in place.

Sew roll-neck collar seam, reversing seam half way so it will not show when turned over.

yarns

Although I have recommended a specific yarn for many of the projects in the book, you can substitute others. A description of each of the yarns used is given below.

If you decide to use an alternative yarn, purchase a substitute yarn that is as close as possible to the original in thickness, weight and texture so that it will work with the pattern instructions. Buy only one ball to start with, so you can test the effect. Calculate the number of balls you will need by meterage rather than by weight. The recommended knitting-needle size and knitting tension on the ball bands are extra guides to the yarn thickness.

To obtain Debbie Bliss, Rowan (and Jaeger) or Yeoman yarns, go to the websites below to find a mail-order stockist or store in your area:

www.colinette.co.uk
www.knitrowan.com
www.debbieblissonline.com
www.yeoman-yarns.co.uk

Debbie Bliss *Cashmerino Aran*
A medium-weight wool-blend yarn
Recommended knitting-needle size: 5mm
Tension: 18 sts x 24 rows per 10cm over knitted st st
Ball size: 90m per 50g ball
Yarn specification: 55% merino wool, 33% microfibre, 12% cashmere

Debbie Bliss *Cashmerino Superchunky*
A super-chunky-weight wool-blend yarn
Recommended knitting-needle size: 7.5mm
Tension: 12 sts x 17 rows per 10cm over knitted st st
Ball size: 75m per 50g ball
Yarn specification: 55% merino wool, 33% microfibre, 12% cashmere

Debbie Bliss *Cathay*
A lightweight cotton-blend yarn
Recommended knitting-needle size: 3.75mm

Tension: 22 sts x 30 rows per 10cm over knitted st st
Ball size: 100m per 50g ball
Yarn specification: 50% cotton, 35% microfibre, 15% silk

Jaeger *Silk DK*
A double-knitting-weight silk yarn
Recommended knitting-needle size: 4mm
Tension: 22 sts x 30 rows per 10cm over knitted st st
Ball size: 125m per 50g ball
Yarn specification: 100% silk

Rowan *Big Wool*
A super-chunky-weight wool yarn
Recommended knitting-needle size: 15mm
Tension: 7.5 sts x 10 rows per 10cm over knitted st st
Ball size: 80m per 100g ball
Yarn specification: 100% merino wool

Rowan *Kidsilk Haze*
A fine-weight mohair-blend yarn
Recommended knitting-needle size: 3.25–5mm
Tension: 18–25 sts x 23–24 rows per 10cm over knitted st st
Ball size: 210m per 25g ball
Yarn specification: 70% super kid mohair, 30% silk

Rowan *Little Big Wool*
A super-chunky-weight wool yarn
Recommended knitting-needle size: 15mm
Tension: 7.5 sts x 10 rows per 10cm over knitted st st
Ball size: 80m per 100g ball
Yarn specification: 100% merino wool

Rowan *RYC Cashcotton DK*
A double-knitting weight cotton-blend yarn
Recommended knitting-needle size: 4mm
Tension: 22 sts x 30 rows per 10cm over knitted st st
Ball size: 130m per 50g ball
Yarn specification: 35% cotton, 25% polyamide, 18% angora, 13% viscose, 9% cashmere

Rowan *RYC Cashsoft Aran*
An medium-weight wool-blend yarn
Recommended knitting-needle size: 4.5mm
Tension: 19 sts x 25 rows per 10cm over knitted st st
Ball size: 87m per 50g ball
Yarn specification: 57% fine merino wool, 33% microfibre, 10% cashmere

Rowan *RYC Cashsoft DK*
An double-knitting-weight wool-blend yarn
Recommended knitting-needle size: 4mm
Tension: 22 sts x 30 rows per 10cm over knitted st st
Ball size: 130m per 50g ball
Yarn specification: 57% fine merino wool, 33% microfibre, 10% cashmere

Rowan *RYC Natural Silk Aran*
A medium-weight silk-blend yarn
Recommended knitting-needle size: 4.5mm
Tension: 19 sts x 25 rows per 10cm over knitted st st
Ball size: 65m per 50g ball
Yarn specification: 73% viscose, 15% silk, 12% linen

Rowan *Spray*
A super-chunky-weight wool yarn
Recommended knitting-needle size: 10mm
Tension: 9 sts x 11 rows per 10cm over knitted st st
Ball size: 80m per 100g ball
Yarn specification: 100% merino wool

Rowan *Tapestry*
A lightweight wool-blend yarn
Recommended knitting-needle size: 4mm
Tension: 22 sts x 30 rows per 10cm over knitted st st
Ball size: 120m per 50g ball
Yarn specification: 70% wool, 30% soya bean protein fibre

Yeoman *Cotton Cannele 4ply*
A fine-weight 4ply mercerized cotton yarn
Recommended knitting-needle size: 2.75mm
Tension: 33 sts x 44 rows per 10cm over knitted st st
Cone size: 850m per 250g cone
Yarn specification: 100% cotton

abbreviations

alt	alternate
beg	begin(ning)
cm	centimetre(s)
cn	cable needle
cont	continu(e)(ing)
dec	decreas(e)(ing)
garter st	garter stitch (k every row)
foll	follow(s)(ing)
g	gramme(s)
inc	increas(e)(ing)
k	knit
m	metre(s)
m1	make one stitch by picking up horizontal loop before next stitch and working into back of it
mm	millimetre(s)
p	purl
patt	pattern
psso	pass slipped stitch over
rem	remain(ing)
rep	repeat
rev st st	reverse stocking stitch (p all RS rows, k all WS rows)
RS	right side
sl	slip
st(s)	stitch(es)
st st	stocking stitch (k all RS rows, p all WS rows)
tog	together
WS	wrong side
tbl	through back of loop(s)
yfwd	yarn forward
yon	yarn over needle

acknowledgements

My personal thanks and appreciation go to the exceptional people who have collaborated to create this book.

The team at Quadrille Publishing, especially Editorial Director, Jane O'Shea, my mentor, for her constant encouragement and style. Creative Director, Helen Lewis, for her tireless innovation on each new project. Lisa Pendreigh, my wonderful project manager for her rigorous support and inimitable professionalism.

It has been a privilege to have Katya de Grunwald photograph this book; her exceptional and distinctive work, together with stylist Beth Dadswell's unique and inspirational concepts have surpassed my wildest expectations. Thank you also to Anita Keeling our fabulous make-up artist and the stunning model Amy Browne at Premier Model Management.

My heartfelt thanks to Sally Lee, my brilliant project maker, for her constant support, enthusiasm, expertise and friendship. And of course Eva Yates and Sally Harding for their inestimable and meticulous hard work in pattern checking.

Stephen Sheard of Coats Craft UK for consistently championing me and Kate Buller, brand manager of Rowan Yarns and the team for their generosity and enthusiastic support. Also Tony Brooks of Yeoman Yarns for his invaluable assistance.

Finally, this book is dedicated to 'creatives' everywhere who continually excite with their passion for the hand made and who push the boundaries of craft by their enthusiasm and innovation. You are my constant source of inspiration.